To Sylvia ..

Layers

Clint Wastling

Best Wishes.

[signature]

Maytree Press 2019

Published 2019 by Maytree Press

www.maytreepress.co.uk

Copyright © Clint Wastling 2019

The right of Clint Wastling to be identified as the author
of this work has been asserted by him in accordance with the
Copyright, Designs and Patents Act 1988

ISBN: 978-1-9160381-8-9

A CIP catalogue record of this book is available from the
British Library.

Cover image: Rough Sea Sandsend © Ian Burdall

Maytree 009

Printed in the UK by PiggyPrint

Acknowledgements

Thanks are due to the editors of the following publications in which some of these poems first appeared: Aesthetica, Algebra of Owls, Dream Catcher, Marble, The Blue Nib and Indigo Rising.

Avebury was originally published in the Eternal Haunted Summer and won the York Writers Poetry Competition 2002. Moment featured in Three Drops from a Cauldron Beltane Issue. The sum of all our parts was published in the Beakful/Bequé Humanity Anthology. Folly Dolly Falls featured in The Cotton Grass Appreciation Society—an anthology of poems inspired by the South Pennines. Splash Boat was originally broadcast on BBC Radio Humberside.

Collecting Ammonites was shortlisted for The Ryedale Poetry Prize.

About the Author

Clint Wastling is a writer based in The East Riding of Yorkshire. His poetry has been widely published in the UK, Ireland and USA. He regularly performs at literature festivals including Ilkley, York and Fantasycon as well as organising workshops. His debut novel, *Tyrants Rex*, was published by Stairwell Books. Clint is currently working on his next novel, *Stalin's Bear*, due for publication in 2021.

To Brenda, Matthew, Eleanor & Amelia.

Contents

Acknowledgements / About the Author

Lazy Shaving	6
Folly Dolly Falls	7
Fossil	8
The Splash Boat	9
Bricklayer	10
Sunk Island	11
Sorting	12
San Nicolo in Carcere	13
At Paulilles	14
Slide Show	15
Manatees	16
Collecting Ammonites	17
Avebury	18
Serrabone	19
Gaveston	20
The Admiral von Tromp	21
Quartz	22
The sum of all our parts	23
Moment	24
Birthday Party	25
Roos Carr Figures	26
Belshazzar's Feast	27
The fading pop star	28
Poison	29
Brimstone	30
Laminate	31

Lazy Shaving

A man should meet his maker clean shaven.
Dad's aphorism born from the sentiments of his time,
hid the bitter irony: one shave begets two
and drags you in.

The bathroom windowsill possessed ritual items:
a safety razor, badger hair brush, soap bowl,
add hot water to the sink, wipe steam from the mirror,
prepare.

Sometimes I'd watch as his blade skimmed
over his tightly stretched skin,
revealing a smooth new surface
as contours were cleared of stubble.

I picked up where dad left.
I wanted side-burns like my heroes
Jason King, Richard Rowntree
and a host of pop stars dressed in flares.

'Lazy shaving,' dad said in judgement,
but this was 1975 and the world beckoned.
He taught me how to use a styptic pen,
which aftershave to wear in moments shared.

When I look in the mirror now
I see aspects of dad, his dimpled chin,
wrinkles reflecting my aging,
an outline fading through deepening steam.

Folly Dolly Falls

Birdsong drowns out gurgling water
and on a cold February day
the walk begins near a railway track —
investment too late to save the mines.

The path hugs the gorge
from which trees cling, supporting
a hierarchy of lichens, mosses, ferns.
All is green despite the penetrating cold.

Layers of sandstone faulted against shale
controls this landscape,
channelling the course of roaring water,
which drowns out birdsong.

In the dank, irriguous domain
I clamber mossy outcrops for photographs.
Here nature hushes human voices
joy and hope remain.

Fossil

There is something military about the waves today,
Uniformly attacking, grinding the applauding pebbles.
My eyes pick out a fossil preserved in fallen rock,
A spiral of immortality, decay in andante.

I wish I were a Mesozoic ammonite charting vast
Tropical oceans in search of food, a mate and meaning.

Waves whisper to the wind which caresses my skin.
Shore and sea with my thoughts lying on wave crests
Drawn then dashed, drawn, diminished again.

Saint Hild froze heathen snakes in your form.
Darwin saw your evolution from great sea-worms.
Children sell you to shop weary tourists,
But I imagine you alive in Jurassic oceans
Knowing nothing of extinction, men or gods.

The Splash Boat

Not one, not two, not three, not four
but five generations awestruck by the gravity
of this mechanism.
To queue and climb the steps
We choose our seat and wait with trepidation
between heartbeats.
Movement slowly accelerates,
the roar of wood on rail accumulates
and screaming punctuates
descent
until the nose plunges and the plume of water
arcs and thrills
drop by drop
onto us
our neighbours,
mums and dads
clandestine lovers.
Finally the vessel judders.
The splash boat hauled to home by jute
we disembark
to watch the next crew
ride the water chute.

Bricklayer

English, header, stretcher, Flemish bond,
he taught me the basic stack before a brew
of builder's tea and a fag break drew all to
the Portacabin.
If he could lay five hundred bricks
he'd get a full day's pay.
Through all but the worst of weather
he'd work long hours, fingers taped,
shammy gloves kept out the lime,
bed of mortar, brick, tap, level.
He could halve a brick with one rap of the trowel.
Before he died,
dad listed houses, bungalows, schools,
a cold war bunker
but his first, he spoke of fondly,
flats on Bricknall Avenue whilst
apprenticed to old Jack Mather.
Perhaps he thought we'd photograph them all.
Make the mortar
mix sand and lime: 3:1 – blend in the water.
I see him now, his thin frame,
a shock of auburn hair
and fingers which
built brick on brick to house his every dream.

Sunk Island

When I first came here, it was the name which made me divert.
Sunk Island, the long, straight, the level of land
my father sought in laying bricks or wood on solid ground.
By some quirk of fate I found ancestors toiled these fields
reclaimed from saltmarsh to feed and fend for families.

Great engines send vibrations across The Humber
as I witness transport at its most gargantuan.
At the horizon, estuary becomes sea
and the world is flat beyond embankments,
drawing the eye from Grimsby's tower to Humber Bridge.

Voices carry across the landscape: fishermen, skylarks, hounds.
There is no silence, no stillness, no rest,
the slow movement of ships; slow movement of tides, clouds.
All this reclaimed from estuary. Nature has her ways
to edge us back, to bind us to the natural course of land.

Sorting

When I walk by The White Horse and Griffin
on Whitby's old Church Street
I remember trinkets found
when mum downsized to a retirement flat.
She snatched the box from me.
You can't throw that!
This will give you some idea of our task:
place card holders, a receipt for grandparent's honeymoon
dated 1935, confetti, a tarnished lapel pin.

Throwing away the past can be cleansing,
can be painful, always a little loss
and if we are preservers of the past
then I am growing toward mother's view:
let others decide, let the future obliterate.
Letters read again, photos seen,
all the love there was evidenced
in all the love there's been,
spent in a million kisses

a hundred thousand wishes
preserving all that's gone before.
Names from this box of trinkets.
Now when I walk by The White Horse and Griffin
on Whitby's old Church Street,
I remember that hotel bill and pause —
my grandparents walked through these doors,
took their honeymoon here
where past and present meet.

San Nicolo in Carcere

It was a hot afternoon, the birds had gone
and cats stretched out sharpening their claws for another kill.

We waited for the bus, our necks and arms
unprotected from the red hot daggers of the sun.
You recommended shade, I suggested the church,
so we moved from light to dark like figures in a Caravaggio.
Inside, the cool played over us
and we forgot our cares behind the Della Porta façade.
The guide, who had been reading poetry by Virgil,
put down the book, asked if we'd like to step back in time.
I joked that if only we could know the ending
before the beginning we might be better informed!
So we descended, taking the chill with us,
and stood on travertine blocks below great columns.
It seemed obvious now, those pillars we counted
in the walls were older than San Nicolo in Carcere.
Two metres below the lectern were temples to Fortuna,
Juno and Janus.
Ionic pilasters rose to the left of us, Doric to the right,
between, niches filled with bones
told of the two faces of that ancient god: peace and war.
I remembered why the bus was late: the demonstration,
flags unfurled for *Peace* and cries for the temple to be closed.
In building San Nicolo truth was built on truth,
until one concealed the other. Where should I find it now?

It was a hot afternoon, the birds had gone
and cats stretched out sharpening their claws for another kill.

At Paulilles

A bay is a bay and beach a beach
until you've seen Paulilles.
Here on the Côte Vermeille
beauty is surprising
given its history
as a factory site
sheltered between the mountains.

Alfred Nobel made
dynamite from nitro-glycerine here.
The chemical name was never mentioned.
This liquid maimed and murdered workers.
It made their hearts race
to a premature death.

Once production stopped,
Nobel's gardens were restored.
The sea became a marine park.
Now we can snorkel on reefs rich with life,
or swim to the platform
like a latter-day Grant and Kelly.

Nitro-glycerine under the tongue
kept Nobel alive a few more months.

Here we lie on the edge of
the Mediterranean Sea,
inheritors of the past
with this transformation.

Slide Show

An image of grandad smiling
at my sister's christening.
Here it is! I remember him old,
smelling of tobacco and peppermint,
always a white shirt, black suit, dark tie.
He was the age I am now
but I remember in a tantrum
mustered by a seven year old
told to go to bed.
I wished him dead.

A widower from fifty,
a lonely man who wanted love,
whose weakening heart
and bronchial lungs
made him fearful, angry.
Now I wish I'd never said
I wished him dead.

In this slide he stands proud,
shoulders back, enjoying the moment,
with *Brylcreemed* hair, looking dapper.
I am playing with a train by his feet.
Can we undo what we say?
No amount of wishing can ever
take me back to that day.

Manatees

Sunday early: clouds building,
a little light rain on a warm day
gave us a rainbow
to remember those murdered in Pulse.

Manatees swim round Portosueno
oblivious to the diving pelicans,
scalding gulls,
baying of dogs drives them to submerge.

Later, they resurface,
noses twitching, snorting
as they graze the narrow channel,
their ghostly outline becoming

more solid, betraying their size,
their sense of fun, rolling,
flapping a fin,
gliding into dark waters.

A mermaid tale rises in salute
and they are gone.
And they are gone
the forty nine

into waters darker than the Styx.
The manatees swim unseen,
ghostly outlines fading like
the colours of aging photographs.

The rainbow shifts into focus
as the rain stops
for whom does it signal hope?
Only those alive to see.

Collecting Ammonites

Hunting fossils with my son on Speeton Beach,
Moving carefully from clay to shale to sand,
Seeking ammonites within reach
Of the searching fingers of an outstretched hand.
Beneath precarious pinnacles of clay,
First fragments then the whole delightful swirl
Of shell emerged once more into the day,
And washed in waves its shape unfurls.
My son's bright eyes and grimy finger nails
Show delight in what he's found.
Chalk cliffs loom and steal remaining day
And rising tide takes all which might be drowned.
Long dead creature turned to stone
How many years have you endured alone?

Avebury

Sometimes with a well-lit moon
I drive across the quiet downs
to this tranquil place with a
slow double bend.

It's easy to linger here
with the main beam catching glimpses.
It is so easy to linger
with night descending
and a slow haunting
communion throwing the dreams of millennia
over crystalline shoulders.

The horned god Cernunnos
and all the forgotten pantheon
slide resolutely between the silhouettes
of the great stones
who echo to many memories.
Sing! I implore you sing.
Wind up the mystery
with a few gentle notes of night
and thoughts of the past,
of times forgotten and sung of now
in dreams of the drive across the downs
to this quiet place.

Serrabone

The bells of Serrabone
accompany the ghosts of
Cathars who fought in vain for faith,
Catalans who fought for freedom
and still hope.

I sit in the cloister
fatigued by heat,
marvelling at marvellous carvings
of centaurs, satyrs and gryphons,
of St Michael slaying the dragon.

The chimes of Serrabone
escort my thoughts
to the summit,
revealing my place in the world
and which dragons to slay.

Gaveston

i.m. Piers Gaveston 1284-1312

It's not a ghost
which haunts these battlements
but love remembered
by the castle's stones.
Here Gaveston said adieu to Edward.
Made lord of all he surveyed by his king
and like his sovereign, master of nothing
except a keen blade,
food,
a week's supply of water.
Nobles would pay to see him hang
or worse being drawn and quartered.
Cliffs,
the edge of life
not its end.

He could throw himself from the precipice,
he could wade into the sea,
neither would kill his love.

The sun is a golden crown of thorns
whose rays pierce.
Herring gulls screech like dying criminals.
These stones hear it all, remember it all,
the good live and die, the bad live and die.
Priory bells toll equally.
The relentless sea blasts below
and Gaveston watches horizons
for a sign of his returning king,
watching from these very stones.
Love or the sword's edge
he was master of neither.

The Admiral von Tromp

They were local men
aware of tides and currents,
so why steer towards
Black Nab, the bleakest sentinel?
On a calm high tide a boat
might pass between stack and cliff
but in fog,
driven east, deliberately driven to the rocks,
there was no hope.

Oh! Alan. Addison said in shock,
his fingers searching the night for phantoms.
They were local men and knew the moods of the sea
but not the moods of a man.

What the hell! Taal screamed.
It was too late.
The hull peeled open,
Admiral von Tromp listed, scraped the wave-cut platform,
lodged; a wrecked ship casting wrecked lives into the fog.
Addison drowned in the wheel house, Eves slipped to the bay.
Whatever happened that October night
no one ever said.
They were local men and afraid of the dead,
of the spirits never quite out of sight.

Quartz

Every beach around the world
possesses your fine grains.
Electrons shared in covalent bonds
allow oxygen and silicon to correspond,
surviving eons from Hadean to Quaternary.
Rock, weathered rock made sedimentary,
reheated and recrystalised,
recycling molecules ancient as earth.
Quartz or sand on every beach,
The rock of ages of which we preach.

The sum of all our parts

Why don't we sing with the dawn chorus?
8000 generations have gone before us
until the threshold of an ancestor
crossed from Homo sapiens to Homo ergaster.
The sum of all who've departed
preserved in all who live today.
Their gift is in our double helix of DNA.
A fragile present.

When I look into the dawn,
glad once more of daylight,
who amongst our ancestors
first heard the blackbird, robin, wren
combine and raise an avian chorus
and who will be the last?

Moment

Walking up the hill from Little Salkeld
with two generations of our family plus one developing.
Enjoying the warm sun we felt impelled
to climb the road, looking for signs, hoping
this stone circle would live up to expectations.
Long Meg and Her Daughters' crystalline
contours are silent witnesses in the affirmation
of spring, praising all that's feminine.
Energy in sound, smell, colour, allow
every living thing to focus on the moment
when the breath of new life ripples through boughs,
twisting the remnants of prayer's atonement.
Long Meg has waited millennia as matriarch of this ring,
I have waited just one season for our birth this spring.

Birthday Party

Only one star followed us.
Great Gran's eightieth and my fifth
coincided that day in 1964.
So we journeyed north by
steam train to Whitby.

Windows rattled, soot landed like dead stars
plucked from the night.
Each time someone got on
draughts attacked our faces, fingers, feet.
Burniston, Cloughton, Ravenscar, Hawsker,
names flew by from dark to dark
and wiping the window revealed
only one star following.

We arrived tired, feet frozen,
to a warm room of rounded faces
holding plates. The smell of candied
fruit and sherry permeated.
I sat on the arm of
Great Gran's chair as the assembled
relatives sang Happy Birthday.
Heat from candles warmed our faces
as we blew out their lights
and made a wish.

Roos Carr Figures

We brothers will row for eternity
long after our lives have become whispers
in the reeds.
If we are discovered what will they understand?
Eight warriors embark. How many find dry land?
Ull the transformer carries us safely across the sea,
his serpent head surveys the shores
where the Parisi hunt, love, live.
We are born naked
and travel naked into the rising sun
armed with shields and spears,
seafarers returning.
As we navigated life
our figures row through death,
carrying our hopes into a new age
bodies long forgotten, wood preserved upon a stage.

Belshazzar's Feast

The writing is on the wall
but not enough people read the words
or heed the message.
The feast continues unabated.
Exotic foods flown from around the world,
Antipodean wines, rare flesh on which to dine.
Standing decked in polyester from crude oil
and cotton from the toil of hungry children,
Belshazzar stands, imagining he's immune.
A man with enough money to feed the poor,
the world has not enough, yet he wants more:
more heat, more light, more meat,
more to delight the senses,
he senses the writing's on the wall,
knows he cannot have it all and continue.
He'd like to save the world
but cannot save himself
without air he cannot breathe,
without water what use is wealth?
So he returns to feast,
the writing on the wall,
ignored by many and by others
never read at all.

The fading pop star

Every time I pass through the deserted station
I think of you.
When the train slows
I see your picture.

You wear a frown
as if you really don't want to be
pasted on a wall so grim and bare.
Dressed in your best
advertising last year's gig,
sold out pasted over dates.
Already corners are peeling,
revealing a well-known cleaning brand.
You float amongst flotsam, *Before the Dawn,*
your life jacket orange,
a reminder of the waking sun,
the passing years,
the cares kindly removed
from your airbrushed face.
The train pulls away.
Tonight I will hear your voice
and remember when we both
were young.

Poison

We made our way down Horse Dale
warmed by early spring sunshine,
saw nothing of hares, rabbits, deer,
seldom heard birdsong
never troubled by insects.

This took a while to sink in.

A day like this should herald
reawakening life
but here nothing lived except
the farmer spraying winter wheat:
pesticide, herbicide, fungicide.

This took a while to sink in.

A good harvest is ensured as
the yield of nature diminishes
and insects head to extinction.
If the food web collapses
this dry valley will remain
as we starve.

This took a while to sink in.

Brimstone

Brimstone equals sulphur,
the hue of rocks in
hills around Vernet,
also the colour of butterflies
rejuvenated by hibernation.
Brimstone Yellows spiral in sunlight
reincarnated in vernal glades,
never alighting to be photographed.
These fractals of sunlight
mirrored our hike
to Pic de la Pena,
their yellow wings as dusty
as the leaves they mimic,
sulphurous streaks
taking a little of hell
to seed hope in heaven.

Laminate

It is the simple things which make me smile,
like my son's handprint preserved in laminate.
It is the delicate things which make me pause awhile,
dew on a web, stars on a frosty night, a love made animate.
The ever changing patterns of a nocturnal sea,
arc lamps capturing stones of the slighted keep,
the touch of skin, the first kiss you gave to me,
I'd run to the sand below but now the hill is too steep.
Yet still sea roars, tides turn, time calculates deceit.
The heart I drew (our initials crossed) has washed away,
our footprints toe to toe are washed away and love's receipt:
our grown up son, rings to check on us each day.
Lives were infinite when we savoured our first kiss
but all that remains is this handprint and time to reminisce.